AF372730

KALEM:

a journey to your inner truth

ISBN: 9789403760452

Cover design: Lenka Dvorcakova

KALEM

It was an early spring when I already knew the essence of my next book, but the title eluded me. Desperation crept in as I yearned for something truly short yet unique. I closed my eyes and implored a higher power for guidance. While awaiting its reply, I began to play with names and letters, seeking a harmonious blend. At last, after mixing names and removing a single connecting letter, I arrived at the word "kalem." Unfamiliar with its meaning, I delved into its origin and discovered its rich significance. Overwhelmed with gratitude, I thanked Source for its divine inspiration.

"Kalem" originates from multiple languages, including Arabic, Turkish, Persian, and Indonesian, where it means "pen" or "pencil." This word symbolizes writing, creativity, and the expression of one's innermost truths. Across cultures, "kalem" has been a tool for documenting thoughts, sharing stories, and exploring the depths of human experience.

The two world wars were physical; this one is spiritual. It is the longest and most significant war in which we all partake – the war between good and evil. Through this book, I aim to assist you in awakening your soul to the potential that's existed within you since your first day on this planet. Like many, I, too, have wandered lost for years, yearning for someone to share this knowledge and liberate me from unnecessary suffering. Finally, I've found my path, and you can too. We're on this journey together, capable of making our world a place that's overflowing with compassion, love, and joy. Therefore, I kindly urge you to approach this book with an open mind and test its principles for yourself. May you embrace the side of light and contribute to the restoration of a long-forgotten paradise.

I have always wanted to change the world and leave a lasting impact. I've hoped that my existence would truly matter one day...

The God within me heard these words and responded: "Your existence matters every single day. Every thought you think, every word you say, and every action you take holds significance. One day, your scars will serve as a testimony that even from the darkest depths, one can always return to the light. Pick up a pen and inscribe all that you've learned, for it may guide others who are lost back to their true home."

CONTENTS

WHO ARE YOU?

There are countless books out there attempting to define who you are, with more being written constantly. As more individuals awaken to their true nature, I feel compelled to share my own insights with you. Personally, I've never been inclined to label myself based on age, gender, or sexuality. After all, how can I accurately express it all when I might have already existed for millions of years, traversing various forms and genders? Objectivity seems elusive; much of what we perceive in life is not concrete fact, but rather assumptions. Identifying oneself solely by name, appearance, or profession leaves something to be desired.

I've often found myself gazing into the mirror, thinking, "Who am I?" In the past, few took the time to contemplate this profound mystery of existence. To many, my introspective musings may have seemed eccentric, leaving me feeling misunderstood despite my efforts to communicate. However, as time progresses, I've noticed a shift in our world. Increasingly, more individuals engage in discussions surrounding their true nature, spirituality, or imagination. Witnessing this fills me with genuine joy. The world is evolving, and I take pride in contributing to this collective awakening and the transmutation of frequencies.

There's always an opportunity for you to join this journey, provided you're willing to embark on your own path of self-discovery and growth. There are numerous practices to undertake before one can ascend to a higher energetic level and wield the power to instigate change. Simply put, you cannot truly elevate the energy around you if you are constantly mired in complaint or feel a sense of lack and injustice in your life. You must first embody what you wish to create around you.

From the onset, my mission wasn't clear to me and I often felt isolated in my desire to discuss these topics. Whenever I broached the subject with others, their reactions were invariably dismissive: "Let's avoid that topic; it makes me anxious" or "Yes, I used to contemplate such matters, but I buried those thoughts deep within to avoid being labeled as crazy." It seemed that discussing such matters was a societal taboo.

Often, I found myself lost in thought, pondering various scenarios about the nature of our world and what truths lie beneath its surface. I asked myself questions like: "Am I merely a character in a movie, surrounded by actors?" or "Could I be the sole existence, with everything around me simply a construct of my imagination?"… even "Am I living within a computer simulation?" These musings frequently occupied my mind, challenging my perception of reality. It all seemed possible to me, yet it felt incredibly lonely not being able to openly discuss it.

The truth is, some people never contemplate such profound questions. At times, we operate like perfectly programmed machines, mimicking the lives of other programmed beings. The typical trajectory involves growing up, pursuing education, establishing a career, starting a family, acquiring property, fulfilling financial obligations, raising children, retiring, and eventually passing away. Anyone who deviates from this path is usually considered unconventional. Now, don't get me wrong; there's nothing inherently problematic with this trajectory, but when it lacks deep love or meaning, it can feel hollow.

Let me pose a question: Have you ever experienced something akin to a sudden surge of divine love, a feeling of finally belonging somewhere? Perhaps it struck you while reclining in the lush grass with the sun's warmth enveloping you, and you sensed the presence of something magical and extraordinary yet beyond comprehension. Then, as you rose from the healing tenderness of Earth's womb and returned to the routines of everyday life, that intense feeling remained, deeply ingrained within you.

I recall experiencing this sensation vividly, yearning for more of it. If it were to return, I vowed to seize it, to embrace it tightly and never release it from my grasp. Deep down, I understood that living an "ordinary" life wasn't my destined path; there was something beyond—a realm of miracles and all-encompassing love—and I was determined to journey there. Before I could propel myself towards that point, depression and confusion were my steadfast companions. I felt like an alien on this planet, longing for my true home as if I had been thrust into a realm where no one could comprehend my thoughts.

Eventually, I found others who shared my desire to discuss such matters, yet our conversations often ended with resigned remarks like: "I know, it's indeed fascinating, but understanding or solving it won't change anything, so why bother? We would only lose our minds." To be candid, I've traversed numerous phases in my life where I needed to lose my mind entirely in order to rediscover it and reconstruct it anew. When we revisit the question "WHO ARE YOU?", I don't intend to convince you that you're definitively this or that, as much of what we perceive are mere assumptions. However, I'm eager to share my perspective in the hope that you might discover your own truth within it.

You and I… we're remarkably alike. We're integral parts of the One, and that One is the God (Source, collective consciousness) that created us. We're not confined solely to our physical bodies; our essence extends beyond them. Contrary to popular belief, we're not powerless to effect change. In fact, we have the capacity to transform everything. The spiritual revolution is underway. This protracted war has endured for too long, but now is the opportune moment for us to reclaim our power and transform this existence as we know it.

GOD

When I speak about God, I never refer to a man whom people pray to in church. Churches are not places I particularly enjoy, as I personally don't feel God's presence there. When I need to sense the presence of God, I go to the forest and feel it in every singing bird, the structure of a pinecone, or the leaves falling from a tree. I often observe these structures and patterns, realizing that mesmerizing connection: the veins of the leaves resemble our own veins, and the branches of trees look like our lungs. We breathe in what trees breathe out, and they breathe in what we breathe out. If you put a pinecone in your hand and look carefully, you can see its inherent perfection. This unmistakable pattern continuously blows my mind. In these seemingly little things, I sense the presence of God. It is something that created us and our entire universe, the fundamental energy upon which every organism operates.

Once, there was nothing, and after the Big Bang, a small singular point was created, gradually expanding into a vast consciousness (God) of which we are all a part. It's also conceivable that something has always existed, without a definitive beginning or end. The concept of an eternal existence remains elusive, and nobody can claim with certainty how it all began. That's why the mystery continues to fascinate me deeply… It's a profound enigma that defies resolution. While we may subscribe to various religious beliefs or scientific theories, insisting on a singular correct answer would be futile. I've come to realize this truth.

Nevertheless, there is something significant that we can do, something that truly matters. We can acknowledge the chaos around us and strive to understand how to navigate the universe, making our lives better and easier by adhering to basic laws and freeing ourselves from unnecessary suffering. In doing so, we have the potential to rid our world of negative energies and malevolent spirits that feed on them. These entities thrive on our suffering, as it sustains their survival. Yet, once we grasp our true essence, much of this suffering can dissipate or be significantly reduced. A friend once shared with me the following: "We are all Gods, powerful creators." You, too, are God, as the moment you were created, this divine energy became a part of you. You are God, and thus, you are more than merely "good enough" – you are powerful.

It's important to understand that God is synonymous with love. Therefore, anything that doesn't align with love isn't of God. The force that brought you into being doesn't wish for your suffering; rather, it aims for you to experience a beautiful and meaningful life. Conversely, dark forces and malevolent spirits thrive on the opposite. Emotions like fear, hate, anger, and jealousy serve as sustenance for them, fueling their destructive influence.

BODY, MIND, AND SOUL

I believe that we consist of three main parts: body, mind, and soul. Some people, perhaps even you, focus solely on the physical aspect of themselves, which is the body. They identify themselves with their name, profession, age, physical appearance, and relationships with others. This tangible aspect feels real and natural to them. The other two parts are often relegated to the background, receiving less attention, but they are just as important as the body—if not more so. Achieving ease in life entails living in harmony and finding balance among these three aspects.

BODY

To enact change in the world, you must first take care of yourself. Every process in your body functions much better with your assistance. When you consume excessive alcohol, energy drinks, coffee, drugs, or fast food daily, your body becomes a toxic environment. Initially, your organism fights hard, attempting to cleanse itself and sending you signals (such as indigestion, headaches, thirst) that what you're ingesting is harmful. Over time, it adapts to this toxic environment and may even begin to crave these substances. I speak from my own experience, as I've also developed many bad habits throughout my life that were challenging to break. Yet, once I made the decision to join my mind and soul so they work together, success became attainable.

On the other hand, drinking plenty of water and consuming healthy food will boost your metabolism and cleanse your organs. You'll feel powerful energy pulsing through every cell of your being. Even if your physical condition isn't where you want it to be or you have disabilities, these factors shouldn't hinder your journey of self-discovery, provided that you choose to prioritize self-care when possible. Still, as I mentioned earlier, this physical aspect must harmonize with the other two parts. So, while you can eat healthily, if your mind is constantly filled with negativity and you are disconnected from your soul, it won't have the same effect. You need to care for all parts of yourself to truly feel your inner power. Of course, I also don't eat only healthy foods (chocolate is one of my guilty pleasures), but I still strive to find a balance. For instance, I might enjoy a coffee with a slice of cake, but I won't indulge in the whole bar of chocolate, followed by two coffees in a row, a pizza, and then washing it all down with an energy drink. Balance is crucial.

You've likely heard the phrase: "Your body is your temple." You are the God, and your body is your temple, so take care of it and learn to love it as it is. Don't try to suppress your authenticity and become someone else. Your creator loves you just the way you are, and if you learn to embrace even the seemingly unlovable parts of yourself, you'll naturally transform them. I used to feel insecure about my body and wanted to change many things about myself. Occasionally, people confirmed my assumptions about myself by saying unkind things about my appearance. These comments deepened my insecurities because, at that time, I didn't have a clear sense of self.

However, everything has changed now. When I decided to take a step forward and work on myself, it transformed my entire personality. My attitude towards myself shifted as I reconnected with my soul. I discovered my true identity, which is why others' comments no longer have the power to influence or hurt me. I respect their opinion, but their perception of my appearance holds no authority over me. I consider myself to be authentic and attractive, especially because of the parts of myself that I once disliked.

People around you can sense this authenticity. If you feel insecure, they will perceive you in the same way, but if you feel confident and unafraid to be your authentic self—regardless of your appearance—they will be enchanted. You will become magnetic and attract far more attention than someone who "looks better than you" but lacks that strong energy radiating from within. With that energy, you can transform all the parts of yourself that you once disliked into aspects you are proud of. They will become your attractive features because your own perception of yourself is what truly works the magic here.

MIND

The most challenging task I've faced in my life has been learning how to control my own mind. In fact, I'm still in the process of learning, and I can't think of anything more difficult. The mind can either be your greatest ally or your worst enemy, depending on what you choose to focus on. You might wonder: Is it even possible to control what we think? It may seem daunting, but the answer is yes—you can decide what to think, although not all the time.

Naturally, there will be moments when random intrusive thoughts arise, but the key is not to become entangled in them. Recognize that they are just thoughts and everyone experiences them. Instead of engaging with them, simply observe them as they pass by. If you find yourself disliking these thoughts, try not to resist them, as this only empowers them further. Instead, consciously generate new, positive thoughts to redirect your focus. Don't entertain your enemies, as they thrive on your attention. Shift your focus to your friends, as they hold greater importance.

Previously, I didn't fully realize the power I possessed and what I could achieve solely with my own thoughts and feelings. In the past, my thinking mind used to influence me, but now, my abilities are growing, and I am evolving into a conscious creator who remains vigilant in observing these thoughts. I function as a protector, intervening in the process of my own thinking if I sense that something is awry. Training your mind is an ongoing process, and difficulties can arise once in a while to test you or help you improve your self-control.

Not long ago, some disturbing thoughts were plaguing my mind, and I couldn't shake them off. The more I tried to rid myself of them, the stronger they seemed to become. What made it worse was that these thoughts began to appear in my reality, fueled by my negative emotions and worries. I found myself trapped in a loop that seemed impossible to break, but then I recalled how far my self-work had brought me, so I resolved to overcome this challenge as well.

While the theory was easy to understand, putting it into practice was more challenging. Every day, I made an effort to focus on my dreams and cultivate pleasant feelings. I wrote down positive affirmations, expressing gratitude for what I have and the aspirations I wish to achieve. Before going to bed each night, I asked my soul to help me overcome my fears while focusing on thoughts and sensations that automatically shifted my mood. Sometimes, I mentally traveled into the past and found situations that evoked intense feelings of love, or I imagined myself in my future dream reality and brought those feelings from there.

When the hands of the clock turned back in time, I found myself suddenly in the arms of my beloved. Once again, I felt every gentle touch, each sparking an electric connection and a warmth that surged through my entire being. With my head lost amidst the lucid clouds, I gazed into those obsidian eyes, finding only love reflected back at me. I also recall a scent that defies description, lingering solely upon the skin of my love. This intense feeling remains the most vivid memory from my past.

Before this love, I often envisioned myself as a child again, playing in an endless green meadow where I crafted delightful meals from grass and mud with other children. Butterflies danced on the breeze, and all kinds of insects were our friends. Those carefree days of youth were a soothing balm for my soul, and I remember that place distinctly. Even now, when I return to my hometown, I occasionally visit that meadow to reignite those feelings. Sometimes it brings a pang of sadness, but I understand that, although I no longer inhabit a child's body, nothing can prevent me from keeping that innocence and joy alive in my heart.

On the contrary, when the hands of the clock race forward unstoppably, the clearest image I carry is of myself sitting in the garden of my own home. It appears as an idyllic haven, surrounded by a tranquil lake, animals, and trees. The entire house radiates love and peace. I tend to it with care, continuing to create art and engage in activities that bring me joy and hold significance. I often relax in my bathtub, gazing through the window into my garden, or I cook a delicious meal and prepare another green tea for the rainy Dutch weather. Then, I sit in my favorite rocking chair and read books by the fireplace. Though I remain unsure of what is best for me and how my story should unfold, I strive to focus mainly on my presence there.

As a result, although upsetting thoughts still arise occasionally, I've managed to redirect most of my attention to uplifting thoughts and feelings. The actions I've taken have lessened the intensity of my negative feelings associated with these disturbing thoughts, so I rarely encounter them in my reality anymore. When they do appear, I simply say, "Everything is well. These things exist, but they have nothing to do with me, and if I don't feed them with my negative feelings, they won't have any power over me. My dream reality is different: breathtaking and magical." Sometimes, I even reinforce these affirmations by looking at pictures of my goals. This practice works for me because feelings of joy eventually dispel any unreasonable fear within me. I have deep faith that by consistently repeating these positive thoughts, feelings, and actions, I will ultimately align myself with my highest timeline.

SOUL

The third part of me is my soul, which I consider to be the most important aspect of my being. It took me almost thirty years to fully reconnect with this profound element. The soul is the true essence of who I am, and it is eternal. While our bodies can be destroyed and our minds silenced, our souls endure through everything, including death.

My soul has been attempting to communicate with me throughout my entire life, using my intuition, inner whispers, and signs. However, I was too attached to my body or mind, so I relegated it to that background I mentioned earlier. Nevertheless, I have always sensed that something was missing, which is why I never ceased searching for answers that could finally satisfy me or guide me back home. Some might say that home is with family, and they are partially correct. While my mother and father gave me life and cared for me, my true creator is something different.

A sensation that I was sent here from afar, with my roots continually elsewhere, has accompanied me my whole life. Deep within, I have always known that I was sent here with a mission to fulfill. Now, I sense my ancestors and guides looking upon me with pride, for at last, I have unearthed my purpose. Returning to Source, I find solace, knowing I am never truly alone. Source and my soul are eternally with me, supporting, loving, and guiding me on my mission. If you feel the same way I used to feel, try to find your way back to them too, for in doing so, you will make a big difference in the world and create something that truly matters.

The best way to reconnect with your soul is through meditation. It involves observing and managing thoughts to cultivate a state of calm and focused awareness. Initially, I believed the main goal of meditation was to completely clear the mind of all thoughts while remaining in a comfortable position. Later, I realized that you can meditate even when you're washing dishes or waiting in line. I remember the first time I successfully achieved something akin to meditation. It lasted approximately 15 seconds, which may sound funny, but it was a great accomplishment for me at that time. Nobody was around, and I was sitting on a hill in my hometown, observing the city lights and movements from above. The sun was slowly setting, and birds were on their way home, forming transient images in the sky. All I felt at that moment was a tangible peace within me. Suddenly, I realized I was fully present, without any thoughts in my head. It felt so freeing to simply flow with everything at that moment. It also was the first step that made me realize I wanted to experience it again, ultimately leading me to further practice.

It might be quite irritating at first and won't take very long, but expect some initial challenges. Still, you can approach it as a hobby or a new language you're trying to learn. The more you practice, the easier it will become. For me, the feeling was so liberating that I craved more of it, so I started to learn how to meditate properly and work with my breath (this is one of the fastest ways to get yourself there). The more you try to stay without thoughts, the more thoughts will come into your mind. That's why breathwork is so important. You no longer focus on your thoughts; instead, you divert your complete attention elsewhere.

To experience this for yourself, take a deep breath in and concentrate on the air entering your nose (you can even count to eight), then hold it for a moment before slowly exhaling through your mouth (counting to eight again). While doing this exercise, become aware of what is happening. Notice how the air slowly flows into your lungs and how your lungs gradually expand. For greater effect, I highly recommend finding a guided meditation video that personally suits you online. Through these exercises, you become more conscious of your own breathing, allowing oxygen to flow more easily into your brain.

During our ordinary day, we don't pay much attention to our breathing, but if we changed that, we could connect to the present moment more frequently and intensely. When you connect to Source, you feel a vibrant energy inside you, silencing everything except your soul, through which Source communicates to you. Simply remain in that deep state of relaxation and listen. It will provide answers and generate healing and protective essence all around and within you. You may also experience blurred vision or tingling sensations in your legs and hands. Some meditations were so deep that upon returning from them, it felt like I was reborn. Magnetism and electricity flowed within me because, in that state, I became one with Source.

With meditation, you will be able to lower your stress levels, calm your organism, heal your body, and empty your mind. It connects you to the most potent and creative force. Suddenly, you will be like an artist facing a blank canvas. It's difficult to freely create artwork when the canvas is already filled with so many layers of dark colors or chaotic shapes. However, you can try to repaint it back to white and start anew or buy a new canvas. You are the artist of your own life and have the power to create whatever you want; you just don't realize it yet.

But firstly, you need to do the hard work, and not many people like that idea. It's similar to finding a four-leaf clover. I have already found hundreds of them because I actually put some effort into it. When people complain that they have never found any, I ask: "But did you actually put some time and effort into it?" Most of the time, their answer is no. Trust me, even if you practice it only for a few minutes per day, over time, you will be able to do it even in crowded places. People will talk in the background, but your mind will be here, now, and empty. You will finally be free to create your own painting, and what you consistently envision in your mind with intense feelings will eventually appear in your reality. These exercises have the power to completely revolutionize your life and enhance it in every aspect. And what could hold greater importance than experiencing a life brimming with happiness? Perhaps not all of you will immediately believe it or be eager to test it, but as it was said to me: "You shall never underestimate the power of planting the seed."

REALITY

I've always been very interested in whether the reality we are currently experiencing is the only one, or if there are more, and what specifically we can call our reality. After many years of contemplation, I concluded that multiple realities exist simultaneously. Sometimes, I sense the presence of my other selves near me. It feels like I am able to travel from one place to another, and things like music, smell, or taste can trigger this feeling. For example, if you used to listen to a specific song or type of music in the past and play it now, you reconnect with that part of yourself again. You can feel all that you felt at that time, and it might bring back an urge to act in a similar way. If you follow through, you'll be on your way to energetically reconnecting with that old self, ultimately leading you to a different timeline. You may also notice an unexplained attraction to certain individuals or things that could be elements from a timeline your current self has yet to explore, but your other self is already experiencing.

Everything is unfolding in the present moment; there is no past or future right now. This suggests that my past self still exists somewhere, but I've opted for different choices, instantly positioning myself in an alternate place. I hold the belief that reality offers the possibility of traversing between these different manifestations of Self. I can go lower or higher; it depends on my life choices, emotions, and thoughts. Lower frequencies can draw me back to where my older version was, which is why I strive to resonate at higher frequencies to align myself with my highest timeline and self.

To connect with your highest self, close your eyes and envision them. What do they look like? Are they doing something specific or dating another person? If you can imagine it and cultivate it in your mind, you inherently infuse that idea with a specific amount of energy, capable of aiding you in manifesting the highest version of yourself and the corresponding reality.

I've continually aspired to be kind, honest, funny, charismatic, strong, and artistic. Now, I find myself already embodying so much of what I've desired, with the potential to become even more. The key is to refrain from comparing yourself to others; instead, compare yourself to your other selves. During moments of distress or insecurity, try to automatically redirect your attention to something positive. Remember who you used to be and who you intend to become. Do you desire regression, or do you strive for growth toward your highest potential? This mindset holds inherent power, motivating you to reject old cycles and past lessons you wish not to revisit. Some situations have a tendency to resurface, almost as if to test us. They serve as a measure to ascertain whether we remain the same person or have evolved to a higher level of consciousness. I find that I am increasingly capable of pausing and introspecting before reacting to such situations, allowing me to observe and understand my internal processes more effectively.

To those who know me well, the following statements may seem a bit surprising, as I have never considered myself a religious person. Going to church has not been my favorite activity, and I've never felt inclined to pick up the Bible. However, upon reaching my thirties, I began to recognize its potential significance, given its widespread acceptance and influence in our world. With a desire to avoid prejudice or ignorance towards something I lacked knowledge about and a wish to broaden my horizons, I decided to give it a chance. To be honest, I didn't read it cover to cover. Instead, I opted to listen to the audiobook and watched the TV show called *The Chosen*, which offers a compelling portrayal of Jesus' life. After immersing myself in these mediums, I found myself captivated by the depiction of Jesus. The Old Testament doesn't resonate with me as much, as the God depicted there is forgiving indeed, but is also portrayed as jealous, angry, and supportive of violence among people. On the other hand, in the New Testament, Jesus is always calm, forgiving, loving, and patient.

As I move forward, I eagerly seek to explore writings about other spiritual masters because I believe that love is the common thread connecting them all. Therefore, whenever someone angers me or a situation provokes a reaction, I take a moment to reflect and ask myself: How would these spiritual masters respond right now? Such introspection often proves helpful, as it underscores the gap between my current state and my desired character, encouraging me to reflect and adjust my behavior accordingly. Responding in a manner aligned with what I believe they would do fills me with a deep sense of love and joy. I find myself much more empowered when I choose calmness and patience in my responses.

This heart-centered behavior can accelerate your journey towards your desired reality because you will resonate at the most elevated frequencies. Make it a point to acknowledge that every day of your life is a gift and feel gratitude for it, as that is how your highest version in your optimal timeline would feel. To energetically merge with this version, you must radiate similar feelings. Give it a chance for one week. Strive to act solely with genuine kindness and compassion, while radiating positive thoughts and feelings. Even after just one week, you'll likely notice transformative changes in your life and being.

EMOTIONS

Controlling your emotions can be very challenging and sometimes even harder than controlling your thoughts. Many of you have likely experienced situations where someone repeatedly tested your patience, got on your nerves, and waited for you to explode in anger. Or maybe you've dealt with people who promised not to lie to you anymore, only to disappoint you by doing it again. But do you also remember someone who gave you your favorite chocolate when you were sad to cheer you up? Or the one who hugged you like no one else, making you feel butterflies in your stomach and the magic of true love? We experience various types of emotions: some pleasant and others not so much. But let me tell you one thing: when you learn how to process your emotions constructively, your life will become much easier. I used to be very impulsive and brutally honest. Most people aren't accustomed to that level of honesty and can easily be offended by my words. Looking back, I see how unable I was to control my emotions or words. However, I also notice a change that has occurred over the years. I strive to improve, and even if I fail and lose control for a while, it now takes me much less time to bounce back to more pleasant feelings.

Self-love has taught me to appreciate my time and not waste it on unnecessary emotions. Of course, sometimes these emotions need to be felt and experienced, but only you can decide how long they will last. When experiencing sadness, anxiety, fear, or anger, try asking yourself if it's really necessary to give them so much attention and time. Yes, I understand that they lied to you again, and it disappointed you, but it's their problem that they should work on and try to solve, not yours. Don't try to change other people if they don't want to change themselves. Only help the ones who show real interest and effort. If they promised not to lie but did it again for the fifth time, do not waste your time, as this is manipulation.

Self-love is one of the keys to complete the transformation of your being. You need to know your boundaries: how much you are willing to tolerate, what actions people can and cannot do in your presence, and how you wish to be treated. For example, some women might convince themselves that being hit occasionally or enduring their partner's screams is justified punishment, or even that they don't mind it. When faced with unkind words or actions, a person with low self-esteem might accept them and believe they are deserved. The worst-case scenario is when these women try to convince those around them, including their own children, that such behavior is normal and acceptable. I understand that in many cases, they cannot be blamed, as they too are victims of violence, unconsciously perpetuating the cycle. This is why learning to love yourself and breaking this cycle is essential.

If someone ever tries to be violent with me or stops treating me in a way that I deserve, we are done. Many people can feel it because my energy speaks for itself.

There is a big invisible sign in my eyes that tells them: I am a very kind person, but do not mess with me. I also used to sacrifice too much in the past, focusing on what others need or want while forgetting that I am the main character of my life and my needs should be more important to me. If you are not happy and your needs are not fulfilled, you cannot truly help or serve others. Taking care of yourself and loving yourself in the manner you desire to be loved is crucial. While you may attempt to love someone else, neglecting self-love in the process can be detrimental, as you may constantly prioritize their needs over your own, potentially leading to self-destruction.

Love is the most powerful force in the universe and, for me, the most beautiful emotion. No matter the question, love is the answer. I always yearned to experience the power of true love. When you gaze into their eyes, your entire world comes to a standstill; you just know that they are what you've always longed for. You recognize their soul and feel as though you've finally found your home. You are parts of the same soul, and you know they were made only for you. There's no reasonable explanation; it's simply the way you feel. And even if you try to maintain your distance, that intense energy still draws you together. Some are fortunate enough to experience this kind of love, but not everyone chooses to follow their heart. There's an array of obstacles when it comes to true love. As Shakespeare once said, "The course of true love never did run smooth." However, you should never stop believing that what is meant for you will always find its way to you, no matter how far it may wander or how long it may take.

In this universe, there are countless types of love, but three of them stand out as the most powerful and transformative: the love for God (your creator, the Source of all energy), self-love, and the love you have for the other part of your soul. This is someone with whom you experience the power of true love. You feel that intense connection because you are both part of the same energetic substance. Despite this, you shouldn't prioritize love for someone else above the love that you have for God or self-love. As I mentioned earlier, God is present in everything in this universe. It operates at the highest possible frequency, and love, being the highest-frequency emotion, enables us to create magnificent things in the world. Another emotion that carries a high frequency and is profoundly potent is joy. Therefore, when you focus on experiencing these two emotions most of the time, you are on the right path to creating paradise on Earth. Additionally, it's important to cultivate gratitude, as it automatically places you in a state of abundance. When you express gratitude, life offers you more blessings to be grateful for.

The most unpleasant emotion you can experience is fear—not hate, jealousy, disgust, or anger, but fear. Love, representing God, creates, while fear, symbolizing darkness, destroys. Far too many dreams and potential miracles have been thwarted by fear. Every time you experience it, question if the situation is truly as dire as it seems. For many people, the most fearful thing is their own death. In that case, it's helpful to realize that your true essence cannot be destroyed; it is a divine energy that can only be transformed. I understand that it may be difficult to contemplate this during challenging times, but the sooner you accept it as part of the natural process, the better. Everything in our nature is born and eventually dies. For me, the discomfort didn't stem from the actuality of death; rather, it arose from the uncertainty surrounding its manner of arrival. Whether it happens in your sleep or it's unpleasant, remember how many painful situations you've already overcome: a broken bone, an unbearable headache, childbirth, etc. Trust me. You can also overcome death, so don't worry about it now. Instead, trust in God's plan and believe it will unfold naturally and for the best. I've relinquished control over what I can't change and focused on what I can. My life rests in my hands, and I'm committed to crafting an unforgettable and awe-inspiring masterpiece. Thus, even my final day won't evoke sadness, as I'll depart knowing I've created something deeply meaningful. I'll leave this planet in peace, wearing a broad smile. By releasing your worries and having faith, you pave the way for your life's plan to materialize. Enjoy every moment of your life, because that's why we are here: to savor, create, and love.

LAWS OF THE UNIVERSE

When I was younger, I believed this world was a chaotic and bewildering place to live in. I couldn't see any order in it, but that's because my own mind was chaotic too. Searching for answers during your teenage years can be tough and confusing, especially when those around you seem oblivious or act as if everything is normal. We live on a planet called Earth, floating in the universe, surrounded by numerous unexplored phenomena, but a great deal of people take this for granted without delving into deeper thoughts. Despite spending years in school, they don't teach us truly essential things like understanding our true nature, controlling our thoughts and feelings, or connecting with our soul. Instead, we're often taught to simply learn and remember certain things and follow specific rules. Do those who stay asleep have it easier? Well, if you wake up and talk about these things, there's a chance you'll be misunderstood or, in the worst case, end up in a psychiatrist's office. Despite this, I believe it's still worth a try.

It took various experiences in my life before I could finally see particular patterns and learn that our universe has its fundamental laws. Whenever I talk about the patterns, I silently laugh to myself, realizing I might sound like a detective in a movie trying to catch a serial killer and slowly losing my mind with all the graphs, signs, and patterns pinned to my board. However, our universe is the most organized organism that has ever existed. You just need to organize yourself first to see it and properly function in it. I personally tested these laws, and my life became much easier from the moment I started following them.

Firstly, it's essential to understand that life mirrors what you project and whether you believe in it or not, karma is real. If you speak ill of someone behind their back, expect the same in return. If you're unkind to a colleague, similar negativity will find its way back to you, perhaps in a different form. Our Earth serves as a distinctive school, one that tests our behavior and character. Taking responsibility for our actions is crucial; we cannot escape the consequences of our choices. The universe operates on the principle of balance, much like a boomerang—what you discard will return to you, sometimes with even greater intensity, to remind you or awaken you.

The encouraging news is that this principle also applies to your good deeds. Help a stranger, and you'll receive similar assistance when needed. Show love and compassion to someone in distress, and more love will flow into your life. Share your resources—food, belongings, and money—with joy, and abundance will multiply in return. Every act of kindness performed with love is acknowledged, so remember that even the smallest gestures matter. When you do good things, there's no need to boast about it to others. Maybe not today or tomorrow, and perhaps not in the way you expected, the rewards will eventually come your way.

Your self-talk is also crucial, as your subconscious mind absorbs everything. If you repeatedly tell yourself that you're worthless, the universe will confirm it. Conversely, if you treat yourself—your soul and the God within you—with respect and love, you will be reciprocated with love and operate as a harmonious team. As mentioned before, Earth serves as a school for us, but it's a particularly rigorous one. When you find yourself repeatedly encountering the same life situations, it's likely you're missing a lesson. Think of it like failing an exam: if you didn't succeed the first time, you'll need to retake it. However, here, there's no room for cheating. God observes your actions, and if you fail to grasp the lesson, you'll find yourself repeating it until you understand its significance. So, if you're frustrated by attracting toxic relationships or experiencing recurring arguments, pause and reflect. These patterns aren't caused by external circumstances or other people; they stem from within. You must learn from them and make different choices to progress to a higher level. Otherwise, you'll remain trapped in these cycles indefinitely.

To invite better things into your life, you need to vibrate at a higher frequency because like attracts like. You may have attempted to attract more love into your life, but if you don't radiate love from within yourself, it becomes futile. Love acts as a magnet for more love. It doesn't naturally flow into the life of someone who is consistently in a bad mood, complaining, or lacks self-love. Even if love does come their way, they may not be able to process it correctly, leading to further pain. This principle of attraction applies to all things that enter your mind. If you desire more wealth, you have to feel wealthy, regardless of your current bank account balance. Don't hesitate to share, think, and act as if you always have enough. The universe will align with your perception of abundance. When you choose generosity, your subconscious takes note and similar blessings flow back to you. To lead an abundant life, cultivate appreciation for every small blessing. Express gratitude in advance for things you don't yet possess, as this mindset can pave the way for those desires to materialize in your reality.

The past few years of my life have been some of the least problematic I've ever experienced. Living in the Netherlands, I have a job that I'm satisfied with. I've also traveled to numerous fantastic countries, have time for my art, and have enough money to enjoy the present. Since learning how to work with and manipulate energy, the things I desire have flowed into my life much more easily and quickly. I now understand that my perspective can greatly influence outcomes. When I quit my job two years ago, I chose not to stress. Instead, I told myself that the people at that job didn't value me enough. I wholeheartedly believed that something much better was on its way to me. I didn't force things and used my free time to write my first book. During this period, I met a man who taught me not to worry about a lack of money and always share a well-cooked meal with others. I recall a time when we were in need of a vacuum cleaner, and he assured me not to worry, as it was already on its way to us. A week later, we stumbled upon an online ad from a woman who was moving and offering her vacuum cleaner for free. Experiences like this prompted deep reflection on the power of our thoughts and feelings.

Despite being conscious of my unemployment and the occasional anxious voice urging me to save more, I opted for a different approach. I wanted to test whether my mindset towards money could indeed influence its flow into my life. Overcoming my fears, even as my account balance gradually dwindled, I continued to purchase the things I needed and wanted. I fostered the belief that money has always been, is, and will always be available.

When the word "money" is mentioned, many people often default to a state of fear. This habit requires a complete restructuring, associating positive feelings with the concept instead. Consider money a source of joy, flowing constantly to you from various channels. I'm writing this because I hope these words inspire you and rid you of unwanted fear. Of course, I'm not claiming to have a pile of money or the ability to buy three new houses, but I'm beginning to realize that manipulating energy is much more important than money itself. Live in the present, embracing it to the fullest, and avoid dwelling excessively on the future or concerns of scarcity. Maintain a high energy level, and money will naturally find its way to you. Many people spend their lives working tirelessly and fixating solely on scarcity, which often leads to growing shortages and increasing debts.

It's crucial to acknowledge that while thoughts and feelings can influence situations, outcomes may not continually unfold as anticipated. The universe operates according to its own laws. For example, even if you're actively trying to attract a specific person into your life, they may currently be involved in a karmic relationship where they need to fulfill their role first. Another possibility is that your specific person is not meant for you, but for someone else. You should never try to draw someone by force or against their will. What is meant for you will naturally align with you based on a similar frequency and in divine timing. Every time you wish for that person, it's essential to add that you only wish for them if it's for the highest good of everyone involved. Source possesses all the information in the world and knows what is best for you, so trust the process, relax, and allow it to bring you what you truly deserve.

We are all made up of atoms, so at our core, we are energetic beings who are part of the One—call it whatever you want: God, the great collective consciousness, or energetic Source. We possess this energy within us that connects us all, and what you feel can have an impact on others. If the majority lives in fear and paranoia—whether it's about catching a virus or their country being destroyed by politicians—it can be challenging for the rest to maintain positivity in the world. Our thoughts and feelings shape our reality. Sometimes, just one person can influence a hundred others around them.

Let's say a situation arises where it's announced that someone at your workplace has a dangerous virus. This situation could unfold in various ways. There might be someone who starts spreading doubt and causing unrest. If others are not resilient enough to withstand such manipulation and negative energy, it can lead to real chaos and disaster. In such a case, it is very likely that the group's thoughts and feelings will form the worst scenarios, causing most people to lose their composure and possibly even get infected with the virus. I am convinced that if the situation is handled calmly, and people in the group help and reassure each other that everything is fine, the collective thoughts and feelings will produce a much more acceptable outcome. Fear can spread like wildfire, but so can love.

The collective consciousness is influenced by us and reflects the world that we create. Instead of persistently complaining about a specific situation, try shifting your perspective and investing energy into personal growth. You'll come to realize that what occurs in your inner world holds greater significance and can bring about genuine change. When the greater part of the world's population adopts a positive mindset and emits love into the universe, the collective consciousness will be able to shape a world akin to paradise. We were born to experience this paradise, and if you understand that there is always enough for each of us and you can attract it into your life with your thoughts and feelings, no politician can disrupt your peace. Let them be and live your life. Karma applies to everyone, and they may have already endured more suffering than you can imagine, even if you cannot see it at the moment.

MESSENGERS AND SIGNS

The universe is constantly communicating with us, even when we're not actively listening. Often, we overlook numerous valuable signs and warning signals. Sometimes, it takes weeks, months, or even years before we grasp their significance. In those moments, we might not have been sufficiently present to recognize and interpret them. Nevertheless, we can train ourselves to be more attentive and aware, not only of signs but also of significant individuals or messengers we encounter in our lives. These messengers appear to teach and assist us. Each of us serves as a messenger for someone else, as we are all interconnected and operate within a shared energy field. Some individuals have a deeper impact than others.

I once shared a living space with a young man with whom I connected on a meaningful level. There was no feeling of being misunderstood because we both resonated on a similar frequency. We were drawn into each other's lives to exchange specific information and knowledge. Despite our frequent arguments, I will never regret meeting him because I learned a great deal from him. Our conversations delved into significant topics such as God, miracles, numbers, signs, and the workings of the universe. He explained that we would always seem foolish to those who remain unaware, yet we possess the power to effect change in meaningful ways. At times, I would find him in the living room jotting down notes about numbers or crafting facial masks from blended fruits, and such moments never failed to bring a smile to my face. He often emphasized the importance of following one's intuition. Others akin to him crossed my path who significantly contributed to my growth and transformation.

Before him, there was another man whom I'll never forget. He attempted to understand me from the very beginning, emitting such intense energy that I felt somewhat intimidated—a rare occurrence for me. Every word he spoke seemed to resonate deeply within me, enriching my spiritual awakening. My journey of awakening had already begun long before, but he played a crucial role in expediting it and filling the gaps I had at that time. As our paths diverged, I continued to diligently work on myself. Eventually, everything he had said resurfaced, making complete sense to me. After a few years, we crossed paths again, and he noticed the transformation within me. His pride was unmistakable, and the moment was incredibly powerful for me.

Around the same time, a woman entered my life, for whom I will be eternally grateful. Meeting her helped me understand the profound meaning of unconditional love. She may not even realize her powerful role in my life, but I do. All these individuals share a common thread: they had the ability to affect me like no one else before. It all unfolded so suddenly, simultaneously, and intensely. We frequently encounter individuals who can influence us, but encountering someone who can communicate with us even without words and touch our soul is exceedingly rare.

Signs surround us constantly, but they aren't always glaringly obvious. When I find myself stuck in life or faced with a difficult decision, I ask for a sign. The divinity within you continually listens and is present to guide you. If you demonstrate honesty or genuine remorse for past actions, it will send you a sign and assist you in finding the right path. Your prayers hold power and are answered if they are sincere. You cannot deceive the divinity within you; it senses and understands everything. I recall numerous instances in my life when I didn't even need to voice my prayers and wishes for them to be heard.

To this day, I remember that cab driver who stopped in the dead of night and graciously drove me home despite my lack of funds, or the employee who swiftly helped me secure a new job and accommodation when I was in need. Before, I took it all for granted and attributed it to coincidence, but now I realize it was God's presence every time. That loving energy has saved me countless times, yet I've never fully grasped why. I used to ask myself: Do I genuinely deserve this level of protection and assistance? Am I uniquely significant? Can I truly impact the world? While I can't provide definitive answers to some questions, I feel a calling within me that grows louder and louder—a persistent drumbeat that cannot be silenced.

A few days ago, I stumbled upon an item that likely belonged to my housemate. Interestingly, it was the same item I had once given to someone I deeply care about. Feeling nostalgic and pondering if the person still thought of me, I decided to ask the universe for another sign. The next morning, as I opened my eyes, I felt a gentle breeze caressing my skin, slipping through the open window and causing a small paper to flutter off my office table. Scattered across the table were around ten small papers, each adorned with various notes. After a moment, I rose and approached the table, picking up the one that had fallen. When I glanced at it, one word caught my attention—the name of the person I had asked about the previous day. The name was part of a note I had written a few months before, as I often jot down my thoughts and experiences. Nevertheless, the entire situation felt wonderfully magical.

This is precisely what touches my soul deeply. I thrive on divine communication, miracles, and the love that envelops me every day, reassuring me that I'm not alone. That's why I urge you all to open your eyes, mind, and heart. Strive to reconnect with your soul and be more mindful, and I promise that you will ultimately discover what you seek and desire. And it's at that moment when real magic will begin to happen before your eyes. You'll finally sense the power within yourself—the power capable of illuminating everything around you.

ABOUT THE AUTHOR

Lenka Dvorcakova, a native of Eastern Slovakia, nurtured a creative spirit from an early age. After graduating from the Faculty of Arts at Presov University, where she studied Slovak language and literature, she took a bold step and began a new life in the Netherlands. Inspired by change and with a deep perspective on the world, she wrote her first book in English, a collection of short stories titled *Crazy Game Called Life* (2022). The stories carry a touch of dreaminess, spirituality, and sci-fi. Dvorcakova draws from her own life experiences, as well as from books, movies, and series that broadened her mind and offered new perspectives on the world.

A year later, she published a poetry collection, *Words and Images* (2023), which is divided into two parts: Awakening and Love Poems. Notably, in addition to poetry, the collection features many artworks she created over the years. Her latest book, *Kalem* (2024), is written in both English and Slovak, reflecting her aim to reach and inspire a broader audience. *Kalem* is a heartfelt testimony of a challenging life journey, spiritual growth, and the search for the meaning of life.